RAVEN INTRODUCTIONS 4

for Liam Miller

RAVEN
INTRODUCTIONS
4

Raven Arts Press / Dublin

RAVEN INTRODUCTIONS 4
is first published in 1986 by
The Raven Arts Press
P.O. Box 1430
Finglas
Dublin 11
Ireland

All poems, fiction and drama © their respective authors, 1986.
Translations © Michael O'Loughlin.
The translator and publisher would like to express their thanks
to the estate of Gerrit Achterberg.

ISBN 0 85186 014 2

Raven Arts Press receives financial assistance from The Arts Council
(An Chomhairle Ealaíon), Dublin, Ireland.

Designed and edited by Dermot Bolger.
Typesetting and make-up by Máire Davitt, Vermilion, Dublin.
Cover design by Jon Berkeley.
Printing and binding by The Carlow Nationalist.

Contents

GREG DELANTY

GREG DELANTY was born in Cork in 1958. He edited the magazine *Quarryman* while in UCG and in 1983 won the Patrick Kavanagh Award. In 1986 he was awarded the Alan Dowling Fellowship in the United States and his first collection, *Cast in the Fire,* from which these poems are taken, is published this autumn by The Dolmen Press.

Tie

Without asking, you borrowed your father's black tie,
Sure that he had another black tie to wear
Should some acquaintance or relation die.
But had he? He should be here somewhere.
But where? Could he be at home on this dark day,
Ransacking drawer after drawer for a funeral tie?
Yes, that must be what has kept him away.
Though you are sure you saw him, tieless,
Smiling over at you, before you lost him again
Among the keening cortege. Leaving you clueless
To his whereabouts, till earth, splattering a coffin,
(Or was it the wind ululating in each prayer?),
Informed you that you can never give your father
Back his black tie, though you'll find him everywhere.

The Beemaster

Without your father and the bees
There'd be no flowers in your garden:
Sweet Pea, Sweet William, Lupin ...
A carillon pealed by the wind
Pulled by slender green ropes,
Only he and the trees hear.
And like the bees, acrobats of the air,
(Let's not forget the bumble-bee.
That aerobatic misfit, defying gravity),
He deplores all swearing and blasphemy.
But you will swear on hearing death bells ring;
Cursing the ancient custom bidding you
Inform the bees *'The Beemaster is dead.'*
Dreading the Queen Bee. Numbed by his death sting.

Ghost Story

Remember as a child how scared you were of ghosts;
Always dispersed by the presence of your father.
But now harassed by his abandoned paraphenalia,
You dearly wish to be haunted by his ghost.
The white, handleless, china teacup
For his false teeth, you still cannot put away.
The shaving brush, flecked with his blood, waits up,
High and dry, on a shelf for him to take up each day.

Today shaving, you recalled how you would scold
Him for confusing his Gilette razor with yours;
How you swore blindly he put his back on your shelf ...
But you found them together again.
Were you to blame yourself all those ghostless mornings?
Or could his ghost really be rambling around?

A Recording Of Not Just Yeats

You heard your father call to you continually,
But you knew that it was all in your head,
Hearing another strange voice repeat
With the nerve-frayed harshness of a tired teacher
To a slow learner: *he is dead, dead, dead.*
But was he? Was your loss tricking your ears again,
As you played a tape for the first time, mike-recorded
Before he died, for you heard him summon you
Over Yeats? His voice had been taped too.

You calmed, sure it was your imagination,
Till you heard him cry *Greg* again, louder
What did he want? Was it help in the garden?
Did he not realise you had been recording?
And as you believed when a child little people
Lived and worked inside radios, full of song,
You are convinced somewhere inside the recorder
You have gone to him and found nothing wrong;
Caught having to help him, amid garden gnomes, forever.

Interrogative

Even the flimsiest, most vulnerable creatures
Are equipped with devices to outwit death:
The night moth blends into its surroundings,
Lichen-coloured, it conceals itself on bark;
Other creatures don the colours of a wasp,
Fooling predators into believing they can sting;
But how could your father outwit death's grasp,
Snatched forever & too soon, under its dark wing,
Always out in the open without sting or cunning.

Street Ownership

Like your father loved to wander off alone
(In an Irish city few have heard of in Norway,
All his light years, till one dark day
He failed to return to his beloved company),
You now mosey off through the streets of Oslo,
Escaping your companions. But even here
The streets, new to you, he can never know,
Are full of his absence. Yet you were sure
You'd escape his lack on fleeing Cork. But no,
No, the streets are no different here,
Except you know nobody & the money
Is more like monopoly money. Wherever you go
He owns every street. His death bankrupts you;
Landing you in jail, with him for sole visitor.

Time Warp

You were smitten,
Eye-tracking
A somehow familiar girl in 40's style regalia,
Stalked by wolf-whistles,
Slaloming down a busy street,
Sidling up a little late,
To kiss her nervous, relieved date,
Your dead father,
Not yet a father.
Sealing more than *their* fate.

Final Warning

Factually your father recalled being beaten
Black & blue by three patriotic Englishmen,
Fighting the evil that was Irish neutrality,
One black-out night in Birmingham.
Then to dispel this memory he gave thanks
To war for the surfeit of unattached women;
Telling story after tell-tale story,
Till the tale of his return to his dying father.
He unwittingly revealed how he must have grieved
In boasting of his vigil by his father's death-bed;
Then as if to warn you, soon himself to be dead,
He reiterated: 'When someone dies, you must continue.'
You've learned nothing of consequence since he has gone,
Except for the fact that you can actually go on.

Leavetaking

After you board the train, you sit & wait,
    To begin your first real journey alone.
You read to avoid the window's awkwardness,
    Knowing he's anxious to catch your eye,
        Loitering out in never-ending rain,
To wave, a bit shy, another final goodbye
You are afraid of having to wave too soon.

And for a moment you think it's the train
    Next to you has begun, but it is yours,
And your face, pressed to the window pane,
    Is distorted & numbed by the icy glass,
        Pinning your eyes upon your father,
As he cranes to defy your disappearing train.
Both of you waving, eternally, to each other.

ASHLING MAGUIRE

ASHLING MAGUIRE was born in Dublin in 1958. Her short stories have been published in *The Irish Press, The Irish Times, In Dublin* and the *Evening Herald.*

SEVEN IN ONE BLOW

Summer is no time to be in Jamaica. Just about everywhere stinks. A welter of heat seeps up through the tar on the road between Montego Bay and Negril. Tyres crack and burst easily. A sticky warmth oozes in your armpits and the small of your back. And the flies, they hop off your nose, they close your eyes. They can make you want to die.

The schoolhouse stands outside the village. Say you are coming down the cliffs from Rick's Cafe, you reach the market-place, across the way you see the Negril Beach Hotel. Follow the road over the bridge past the Hotel Sunrise on the left and the Hotel Sunset on the right. Now stop. That's it, there, on the block of cleared land. The grass is longer than usual. The boards on the windows look new beside the stained whitewash. Coconuts fester on the ground. Nobody goes near the place now. Not since last year.

The kids don't care if a new teacher never comes. Jimmy and Charlie and the boys, they are not interested in all that countin' and poetry and stuff. The parents, they shrug, and say 'What good it goan do them anyway?' But they do care about History. Philip Renshaw discovered that within a week. Not his kind of History, not the explorers and economic expansion, not that, but Rasta History: 'That the one true History, man. The rest all Whiteman shit.' So Jimmy told him one day. That was O.K., Philip Renshaw was a College graduate. He was open-minded. All he wanted to do was write poetry. Man, he sure got plenty time write poetry now.

Last summer was just about the hottest summer anyone can recall. There was no wind. Hotel yards reeked with the rot of empty conch shells. The only thing to do was smoke some ganja, sleep, forget about the heat. That's how it was the day Philip Renshaw arrived.

John de Luis, the taxi-driver dropped him off at the school-house. No-one came out to meet him. When John de Luis drove back through the village later on, the white teacher was still there. He was sitting on his suitcase, reading. This had provoked a titter round the Courtroom.

Philip Renshaw kept to himself. At sundown when everybody went to the beach for washing and discussion, Philip Renshaw stayed in his house. Once Jimmy and Charlie and the boys sneaked up to spy on him. The teacher was at his desk, writing. All of a sudden he jumped up and ran around the room 'like he had the devil in him.' He was trying to swat a fly. 'He done beat them flies till they was dead.' Jimmy's eyes rolled. The bodies in the Courtroom swelled to a great 'OOOooohh' and subsided.

Philip Renshaw worked hard. There was nobody going to deny that. When kids did not show up he went to their homes the same night to know why, Mr. and Mrs. Davis, Charlene and Martha's parents, remembered, 'twice, they was missing from school and twice he come see us,' said Mr. Davis. Her girls were good girls, said Mrs. Davis, and threw her head into her lap to wipe her tears on her skirt. 'They was goan be good women, good wives, good mothers,' the woman moaned.

Nowadays Fred's place is a tourist attraction. Nothing in the ramshackle store has changed since that night. The ceiling-high shelves are still stacked with tins of condensed milk, boxes of soap powder, bottles of Guinness and sachets of Silvikrin. To reach the counter you have to squeeze between hard sacks of flour. Fred will serve your beer in its bottle, setting it down on the scorch-pocked oilcloth. 'Same drink Renshaw had that night,' he will say with a confiding eye. If you take the bait he will call in Mama Fred.

She pushes through the bead curtain trailing fumes of spice and marijuana. Fred retires to the corner and stands stoop-shouldered.

Now and again he nods to confirm a point. The diminutive woman recites her story unchallenged. Occasionally her words slur and she dabs her streaming, bloodshot eyes with a man's handkerchief. When she is finished she waits for you to buy her a drink.

According to Mama Fred, Philip Renshaw came to her place on the night of November 30th, 1979. He had a cold beer. 15 cents extra for a cold drink. It was the hottest night that summer.

18

All the customers paid the extra. Philip Renshaw said 'Mama, I think I'll go to the disco tonight,' and Mama Fred, she said, 'What for you want do that? This night too hot, you only waste your energy.' But Philip Renshaw he didn't listen. He finished his beer and went across to the Negril Beach Hotel.

No-one ever stays at the Negril Beach Hotel. Every morning breakfast tables are set up on the concrete terrace and at midday they are cleared away, unused. The only regular trade is the Saturday night dance. Jimmy and Charlie and the boys went every week. 'Music, that the soul own sound,' Jimmy says. But he has not been to the disco since last summer.

When Philip Renshaw entered, the dancers scattered onto the foam-filled seats. He walked straight up to the bar and ordered a cold beer from Alexander King. This witness went on to describe how Mr. Renshaw rolled up his sleeves and stared into the mirror behind the line of bottles. Gradually the black figures swarmed into the white light again. Bodies bent and worked themselves together. Sweat started to their faces. Dreadlocks bounced. Body smells came in waves against Philip Renshaw's face. Alexander King refreshed Mr. Renshaw's drink.

His lips were stuck with the tang of damp salt. His body began to sway back and forth on the bar stool. His breath came with the pant of the drum. That was when Charlene asked him to dance. She took his hand and guided him down to the dance floor. In the ultra-violet light, only the shapes of white underwear shine. Features recede and eyes and teeth gleam. The sticky closeness of bodies oozes into your senses, seals your eyes and dries your mouth.

Jimmy testified that his teacher danced all night with Charlene. Martha, her twin, danced with Charlie. Outside the disco they saw Charlene link arms with Mr. Renshaw. Martha followed them. This corroborated Mrs. Davis's previous statement that her girls were always together. They shared everything, like good friends.

The Court was adjourned until 3 p.m. The Judge rose. The men and women filed silently out of the Courthouse. Fred pressed an uncomfortable homberg onto his grey head. Mama

19

Fred squinted in the dry light and her crumpled handkerchief trapped a dribble at the corner of her eye. Mrs. Davis heaved her shoulders and a gulp of air locked in her trachea.

Jimmy and Charlie and the boys arched their backs in the sun. Alexander King lit a cigarette for John de Luis.

All through the recess they hung around outside the Courthouse. As if tied to the building by some invisible chain nobody moved more than a block away. The street was hot. Papers and fruit skins shuffled in the dust against the pavement.

The first witness to take the stand that afternoon was the Rev. Bartholomew Henry. He was brought through his account of the events on the morning of Sunday 1st December 1979, by Mr. Fabian Russell, Q.C., Counsel for the Defence. Rev. Bartholomew Henry had been preaching at Sunday School in the Chapel of the Pentecost. The children were commencing to sing Psalm No. 135 when Rev. Henry observed a young man standing at the door of the Chapel. The man was not known to Rev. Henry. He told the organist to proceed with the Psalm while he attended to the young man.

The man's name was Tobias Smith. He was just passing through, or so he told Rev. Henry. He was seeking directions to the nearest gas station. The rear right tyre of his car had burst and he had no spare. Rev. Bartholomew Henry accompanied Mr. Smith to the road, the better to assist him. An intense buzzing of flies distracted them. Even for that time of the year it was unusual. Mr. Smith pointed towards a white object flapping in the grass. And that was how they came upon the bodies. The twins, Charlene and Martha Davis, lay side by side. Their clothes were ripped and folded back like wings. A horde of flies covered their faces. Mr. Smith got sick. Rev. Bartholomew Henry offered up a prayer. From the Chapel the Sunday School voices chanted the lines of Psalm No. 135.

Mr. Fabian Russell, Q.C., Counsel for the Defence, submitted that the evidence was insufficient to warrant a conviction for his client.

The jury withdrew.

A verdict of guilty was returned. Philip Renshaw was sentenced to two terms of life imprisonment to be served consecutively.

Back in Negril Mama Fred, she say 'Man, he sure got plenty time write poetry now.' A torpor has settled on the village. Nobody has woken from the sleeping of last summer. 'But the ganja doan let you forget some things.' Jimmy and Charlie and the boys lie against the coconut trees and talk. The thing no-one wants to remember is the way the girls were found lying in the grass with their heads smashed and their arms and legs all bunched up.

Philip Renshaw has written only one line of poetry in his first year of imprisonment:

'I now have the only flieless house in Negril.'

DEATH BY WATER

In death's hospital the dying shift their bones, releasing from beneath worn sheets their vapours of decay to clog the air in long wards. To go in there is to taste death, the foul traces of nitre linger in the lips and the nostrils, and hang like smoke about the hair and clothes long after the place is left behind. To pass by is to hear the faint moans and spasmodic cackles of men and women at their wits' end, laughing out the last of their life.

Moonlight brings up the bone pale shine of hands and heads. Under the darkness bitter juices seep away, drawing all the nourishment out of the flesh. Moonlight through the windows lays out squares of light on the dark surfaces of the room, a key-board for the march of death. Breaths come, gasps rattle. Moonlight pulls the stops on the pursed mouths pumping a last chorus of breath and breath and breath, arrested only by the unholy high pitch of delirium.

Death, Maria knows, is coming to her. Into her mind run the words of prayers she has not said this long time, the ream of hymns and psalms and paters that she learnt at school all come to her in bits and scraps.

On good days when there is sun and maybe a breeze in the air she can feel her old self inside her. Under the crumpled dry skin she can feel the downy skin of youth, good rounded skin asking to be touched. There used to be days when all she wanted to do was to lie on her bed feeling the comfort of herself closed into her body. Now, Maria thinks, she is like a fruit with an old tough skin on the outside and inside the remnants of her sweet young flesh.

The days are rare when she feels that youthfulness inside of her. After drinking a few scoops sometimes it comes rolling back in on her like a hot tide. Then it rolls out and leaves her dry and lost like an old piece of a shell, and she looks around her like a traveller come back to die in the place he was born only to find that no-one knows or recollects him.

Now Maria maintains that everyone knows the way their death is coming to them. She had it from the cards one time that her own way out was to be by water. All the water she ever sees these days is rain so it will likely be pneumonia that carries her off and not the ocean or the river as she once imagined. For the sea was the most powerful thing she had ever come in contact with, and, sometimes, when she lies awake through the night she fancies that she has dropped right off the earth and feels herself caught in the lift and dip of the waves. She falls to remembering then the first sight she got of the sea, when the young pot-boy out of the hotel that she worked in took her there. She had a white cotton frock on her and a wide straw hat that she got the loan of off Consolata the squinty-eyed one in the flat upstairs.

He brought her on the bus to where the road ended and they walked, holding hands, along a path into fields of tall grass.

'I don't see the sea,' she said.

'You will in a minute,' he told her.

He was right too, for, soon, the path turned and the ground fell sheer away.

'Look over,' he said.

When she looked, easing her neck forward, she saw, miles below, the shifting grey green sea and the spurts of white thrown up by waves against the rocks. The thunder of it stopped her breath.

One behind the other they followed the narrow path along the edge of the cliff. There was no horizon, the sky and the sea had closed together. Neither of them spoke as they walked. In the distance Maria began to see tall shapes like chimney stacks rise up out of the sea. Coming closer she saw that some were joined by arches making windows onto the waters. 'The waves done that,' the boy said, 'broke bits away from the land and made holes in them.'

Although the sun was hidden behind low cloud the heat lifted a haze off the sea and cabbage butterflies darted up now and then out of the grass. Maria's legs grew tired but she was not about to say that to him. He went on walking without looking back. Maybe he had forgotten she was there. She was not much bothered for she hardly knew him and it was only the prospect of a trip to the sea that had brought her out this day.

'Here Maria, look at this,' he shouted of a sudden.

She quickened her step to catch up with him. He was standing at the brink of the cliff where it curved inwards and when she reached him he told her to kneel down.

She placed the hat on the grass and knelt, spreading the skirt of her white dress in a circle around her knees. 'Now,' he said, 'lie down, like this.' Side by side, then, they lay on their stomachs, their heads dropping over the cliff's edge. Beneath them, in the crescent of the cliff base, was a strip of white sand and a bright circle of sea water. In the dizziness of looking down Maria felt the water pull her towards its centre. Out foreign somewhere, her Da had told her, the people maintained there was a magnet at the bottom of the sea. She was afraid of the sea and she was afraid thinking of that magnet.

A mild wind rose off the waves and lifted the loose ends of her hair, rustled through the white layers of her dress and tilted the brim of her straw hat off the grass. Another sudden gust snatched at the brim and flung the hat over the cliff.

'Oh Jesus. The hat.' Maria cried and leaned further across the edge to see it fall onto a group of rocks at the water's edge.

'I'll get it,' the boy grinned.

'You can't go climbing down there. You'll be killed.'

'No I won't,' he said, 'I've done it before, often.'

He jumped up and ran to the side of the cliff, then disappeared.

'Oh sweet Jesus,' she said to herself. 'What am I going to do if he falls and breaks his neck or something?'

She blessed herself and crossed her fingers and propped her chin in the palm of her hands. Nowhere could she see a sign of him.

In another moment the hat was lifted off the rock and launched onto the sea where it circled and drifted out towards the grey deeps. 'Stop.' Maria shouted. 'Stop. Oh suffering Jesus she'll have my life.'

By now the boy was down on the sand, running along, waving at her and pointing to the hat. She laughed at the sight of him so raggedy and small down there.

'To hell with her frigging hat,' she thought, 'she can get another one. Your man's a bit of a laugh anyway, I'll say that for him.'

He was gone again, out of sight. In the distance she saw the lonely hat sailing off.

'Maybe it'll land on a desert island where some shipwrecked eegit will be glad of the bit of shade. Or even it might end up in Africa. I'll tell that to Consolata. That'll make her feel better. She's forever giving money to the Missions for the black babies. Now I can tell her she's sent them a hat.'

The boy came up panting and laughing behind her.

'Here, I couldn't get your hat, so I brought you these.' Bending over her he clapped two cone shaped shells against her ears, like muffs. 'Listen,' he shouted through the roaring sound that rushed in on her head, 'listen to the sea'.

She put her hands over his and he slid his bony fingers away so that she clamped the shells hard to her ears. A mad sound blew through her head like the hissing of the waves but louder. She shut her eyes and felt herself soaring off of the ground. Opening them again she spun in rings. A wind like this must fill the head of a bird she thought, as the cliffs and sand and sea spiralled below, swerving now towards her, now away. She held tight to the belly of the shells and the cliff fell away. Her tongue ran over her lips and tasted salt on a current of air.

When she took the shells off her ears the earth stopped circling and the fields fell the way they were before and the sky pressed low again. She looked around to see where the boy had got to and saw him lying on his side in the grass, his head cocked against one hand, watching her. His other hand plucked shreds of grass and piled them into mounds.

'Can I keep them?' she called, holding out the two white curling shells.

'Of course. I gave them to you didn't I?'

'Oh, I'll keep them always,' Maria laughed and pressed them once again to her ears. 'Whenever I get fed up I'll just lie down and cover my ears with them and forget about everything except this place.'

She could do with them things now, Maria reflects. Still, with the rain coming down without let up or let out she can just shut her eyes and think it is the sea, and maybe cradle her hands around her ears to make the effect of the wind, but it is not the same. The best that can do for her is to keep out the noise of the other old ones on the ward. Where did the shells get to after? That's a thing she cannot remember.

There are mornings when she wakes with the taste of salt on her lips and then she knows she has been back to the sea in her sleep, and she wonders for a moment is she alive or is she dead. Sometimes again she wonders if she dreamed it all in the first place. All she knows is that when she thinks of her death it comes to her like the hundred and thousand years' weight of stones and shells heaped over her body till her own bones are no more than a handful of sand on the bed of the ocean.

MAURICE RIORDAN

MAURICE RIORDAN was born in 1953 in Co. Cork. He was educated — and has since taught — at University College, Cork, and at McMaster University, Canada, from which he received a Ph.D. in 1981. He is now married in London, where he works freelance as a lecturer and writer.

Acknowledgements are due to the editors of *Exile* (Canada), *Irish Press, New Statesman, Poetry Now, Quarry* (Canada), *Poets of Munster* (Anvil/Brandon, 1985), where some of these poems first appeared.

Wet Night

Such a night shelters the eels.
They file through the drenched fields;
cross roads, ditches; coil into pools.
As a child I stoned one, a live
flex in the grass: stilled it.
Something recalled this night.

And a troupe of frogs jumping
across a road, sequinned in the cone
of a headlamp; sliced or crushed
in their caper through the farms;
as eels from Alpine corries seek
the Sargasso, melt into ocean . . .

cheated by continental drift!
A mime that drops below the moon
or any influence of stars
we separate, turned towards sleep,
each in an envelope of wet,
as amphibious shapes converge.

Whistling

When Sailor Flynn, after one too many,
gave his right arm to the teeth
of a spinning flywheel, the Navy staunched
the blood, sewed up the stump

and sent him back where he belonged —
on top of tractors, under combines
and dung-spreaders, searching for
elusive nozzles with a grease-gun.

He drank no more. Instead he took
to calling on the wives of farmers
after dark; but never forgot
the rhythm of the licensed hours.

You might catch him near midnight
whistling past the graveyard,
raising an empty sleeve
in salute to his buried hand.

Facade

The massive doors of the jail
where my dad spent time
close forever, beside them a plaque
that bears the names of fellows
shot in '20 and '21.

Were I to pass through there now
I might find myself in a lab
of the New Medical Wing,
but not the cell where — so he said —
he got his education.

A week's diet of bread and water
was his prescription for a free
and easy world, since the day
he walked out with a full beard
and a lifelong craving for sugar.

Nickname

The windows of the Great House gave
onto a sloping lawn with avenue
that curved like some noble gesture —
up which Grandfather was trotting
his barouche in 1884-or-so,
when Lady Standish Barry cried out
'Oho, look at him — the fine buck
coming to have his rents reduced!'
And Standish had the first motor car
in County Cork, registered no. 1.
Joyriding from town that first day
he killed a sheep and pair of lambs,
but the next morning he was in
that passage there with three hoggets.
So said my father on Sunday morning
as he brushed and brushed his shoes,
blacked the night before, until they shone.

Missing Sire

1

The telephone poised,
loaded with summons;
tonight the grinning
court of dream . . .

2

I am turning in my first damp bedroom;
Father is away; the car roars home,
driving fast in second gear: is it him?

We are bending — the three of us — where
he has fallen dead drunk on the threshold;
but no, he is weak; pitiful, he is dying.

(The cry of a life held in wilful hands
to be crushed or to be kept: forgive me)

Too late; a blue wind out of the east blows
against the house: *get inside, get inside.*
I am fastening doors and windows.

No use, the years reel in silver terror,
and the cry from the kitchen is caught
in the screeching abroad where he is gone;

she turns away in final disappointment;
waking then, I hold for a second
the stone of fate in my closed left hand.

3

So to the room.
Where he lies past
all embarrassment of intimacy
or reserve; no effort now
to please or know him.
Reduced, a certain task,
the weight he has left us with.

4

Neither to please or know
a dream I had:
              You were
a dark-browed Catalan poet,
fighter, man-of-the-people
in the old days; your face
told of honourable failure.

How did you dream me, if ever —
set on a colt, hands held down,
toes in, riding from the knees;
lissom, erect; your tall son?

The Ladder

Each year a foal was born my father stuck
the mess of clearings on a length of furze,
then draped them from a rafter in the shed
beyond the reach of cats and scavengers.

No-one cared to ask him why he did this.
It seemed he had a notion the array
of skins — as unsightly as hanging bats —
kept count of all the foals born in his day.

Not that he'd expect anyone to count,
since he was well aware a time would come
when the rafter would give and, at a loss,
some carpenter might throw them on the dung.

But they are still there, obscured now with webs
and swallow droppings, of no consequence
to man or beast, feeding only the weevil
or whatever is nourished in this silence.

I've poked a chance stick into the shed's gloom
and have, accidentally, dislodged the crust
of one: which hardly startles the shy foal
curiously alive in morning frost

nor wakes my father's heart at such a moment
nor tells me who I am, yet I invent
a treacherous ladder and duly hang
the afterbirth where it seems to belong.

El Dorado

It was to be your first stroke
on the fair way to success —
the caravan we did up that spring
and towed the back road to Ballybunion.
You hadn't bargained for the lady dentist's
propriety about bed linen or the mess
could be left by a whirlwind weekend;
or the wagon train of depressions across
the weatherman's chart all of August.
So I became your solitary guest
and caretaker, guttling Agatha Christies
to the flutter of gaslight, my pallor
doubled in the rain-specked glass.
I uncovered a nest of drowned larks
on the fourth tee of the golfcourse
and sat afternoons out on the rocks
to watch the sea coming, coming.

The Doctor's Stone

The Doc, in slippers and samite gown,
serves warmed milk and honey,
rashers, wads of blood pudding,
to cure a night on whiskey.
He's telling of a trip to Achill —
how, as he squatted on the sand,
he saw beyond the ocean's rim
the bright tips of a palm forest.
He never found the spot again
but knows he glimpsed Hy Brazil.
And he takes from a leather case
a stone, the size of a wren's egg,
that three days ago was lodged
inside his kidney. He traces
its passage to the bladder
down the urinary tract
into the palm of his hand.
Gives me the stone to hold.
It is so light and real
it could well be the one
I all but wrested from a dream.

West 25th

(for Sue)

Another of those long weekends when kids
disappear, and a woman you might know
is raped on Main, or someone you don't scales
an office tower with a .22.
No wonder the freeways going North shimmer
and boil with traffic heading for the lakes.

Yet we're half-glad to be left to ourselves
in a suburban drowse, to wander up
a drive where only a video eye peers
into the glare; and we glimpse the better life
if ever a slice of perfect sky should drop
to make a swimming pool in our own backyard.

Night-piece

The night's damp breathing oppresses.
Sleeved in a fine sweat, factories toil;
a hospital, flats — their hot persistence.

Warehouses squat close upon the quays.
For hours I have watched the tide climb
to fulfilment, brimming now at my feet.

A soft explosive, it is pressed inside
arteries of sewers and conduits, weeping
noiselessly upwards to infiltrate sleep.

Pursuit

Still I see you —
white upturned face, small
in a man's dufflecoat.

In how many stations
have you stood, stood and wavered,
stray flake in sleety rain.

Farewell

What happens to beach balls?
A shout sees this one off.

Already winking like a light
on the horizon, unregarded.

That was so used to bright days,
beaches, the laughter of children.

A bubble of air
in a strange element, surviving.

ROSITA BOLAND

ROSITA BOLAND was born in 1965 in Ennis, Co Clare and is a student in Trinity College, Dublin. Her work has appeared in The Sunday Times, Cyphers, The Evening Herald, Poetry Ireland, and in the forthcoming Faber anthology, Hard Lines 3. Her translations from the Irish of Cathal Ó Searcaigh appeared in *The Bright Wave*, Raven, 1986.

Cracking

She keeps her eyes shut all the time now;
So I can't look into her head, she says.

At odd moments of the day
She finds my hand and grasps it hard,
Willing herself to feel a current of life
I know she would drain me if she could
And leave the dry husk
To wither at the end of an arm.

In the seeping blackness of three a.m.
She is way up there in the night,
Swinging the arc from height to height.
Hypnotised, I watch the tossing hair and
The way those bones tremble underneath
The false skin of her muslin nightdress.

She is becoming so brittle
That soon I shall sing too high a note
And she will shatter like glass in my hand.

Debutante

The polished wardrobe doors
Threw their reflection back
In a confusion of mahogany
And the gleam from creamy taffeta.
As she watches the outline of her body
Became gradually blurred
With where the sheen of the wood began.

The night was a swirl of dance,
Pale shapes of long dresses defined
Against the harder colours of black suits.
There were no ragged edges
No colours bleeding into each other,
And tangled up with the smoke and music,
Her hair was the only liquid thing.

In the early morning, everyone went swimming
At a nearby lake, and afterwards
The impressions that stayed with her
Were those of evening clothes in heaps
And white bodies moving in pellucid water.

Skull

(for Ian)

You picked it up and stroked the smoothness;
Polished marble-white skull and I thought
Of Grecian sculptures cool and silent to the touch.

Your crimson scarf gashed the skyline quietly.
I felt the shock of its warmth hitting my face
And a sudden chill shoot through the skin.

Raising my face to the socketless wind,
I flinched as you traced a finger down the cheekbone
Of the skull in your own tender way.

Rain falling slowly in hot, wet drops
Ran cleanly down the drained bone
And spattered like blood on the dry earth.

Behind your funny ears and tousled hair,
I felt flesh and bone, your skull —
                                    My skull.

Gathering Wildflowers On A Warm Day

That day was a jungle pool when
I dived into the cool green shadiness
That rushed above my head as I drowned
In its warmly exotic, Gauguin beauty.

In the fields, the wildflowers
Splashed their strange, startling colours
In brash tissue-paper petals and
Soaked up the sundrops,
Reflections shirring the water
All wet and wrinkly
Like an enthusiastic child's
Crinkly watercolour painting.

Their pollen dripped onto my fingers
And there was a soft oozy sound
When I pulled the stalks
That seemed to wriggle, stuck unevenly
Into big glass jars of tropical jungle
Wavering lushly in the water;
I longed to eat their fresh greenness
And devour the day, stem by stem.

Summer With Clara

Where is Clara now?
Hidden in the folds of her cool linen sheet
That we scribbled on with big coloured pens,
Drawing funny pictures and writing words.

She watches from a photograph on the wall,
Making me remember the days
When she tossed her straw hat across the room,
Ribbons all aflutter in excited little vibrations;
Pulse on pulse — heart on heart.

Love in the sun that burned too warmly
Not to wilt at last,
Like the summer flowers
I bought for you on Grafton Street
(Feeling marvellously gallant?)

But I didn't want to hear the words.
So you wrote them instead on the sheet
All sideways and backways and everyways.
We hung it from the shutters
To keep out the people and the dust.

When you went at the end of the summer,
All you left were your words
Folded away in a drawer somewhere
"Where is Clara now?"

i am not cool, joe

eleven on sunday and i am not cool, joe
though i dip my feet
in the streaming silk of the creek
and watch the water shot reflections
i am not cool, joe

on school sundays we sang hymns from yellow books
and the liquid jewels of the stained glass
splashed mosiacs of colour on bare white walls
which we lived inside in a kind of innocence
where life was as starkly simple
as the monochrome of the nuns habits.

tiled marble corridors made the walls cool
lay your face against them and you were cool too
but we were as warm as we knew how, joe
kindling fires from flints of conversation
that sometimes blazed inside a classroom
within the coldness of white walls.

when we eventually tumbled out the windows
and held our fingers on the pulse of what they
call living it was so hot i dropped it, joe
and it still burns if i stand too close
so i build my own walls of protection and
watch the world through a translation of imagery

the white hot walls of my life hold me inside them
and even colours have changed their language
so i can learn only primitive things of the senses
all five remaining their rich sensuous selves within
the rawness of an intense world no longer chilled
by the marble tiles of black and white schooldays.

eleven on sunday and i am not cool, joe
though i dip my feet
in the streaming silk of the creek
and watch the water shot reflections
i am not cool, joe

Vignette

She is hanging her silk stocking to dry at the open window,
The light a pale gossamer shining through them
And coming into the room, he stands and watches
As she undresses with all the abstraction of a flower
On a still day, gradually shedding its scented petals.

Mother, From Daughter

Wrapped in one of our wide-armed hugs,
i like to think that i am taking
A little of your great warmth
And giving a little back.

Poolbeg

Poolbeg looks for you.
From every picture that the eye frames in Dublin,

P
O B
O E
L G

Rises like quiet smoke on the horizon.

Poolbeg in mist
Becomes pale shapes blending into
Pearl and grey moaning of foghorns
Washing out Dublin Bay
With their echoing shiver.

Poolbeg in sun
Splits the skyline open
With red and white excitement
Throwing out quivering shadows
Of slender fingers on the city.

Poolbeg looks for you.
Glimpsed from somewhere within Dublin,

P
O B
O E
L G

Reassures me that my world has not yet fallen.

Fireworks

We sat with our arms held tight
Around each other
While we watched the fireworks blow open
In huge, coloured dandelion puffs
That burst and fell like melting tinsel
Against the backdrop of an August night.

I knew that those nights
Were climbing into bed beside us,
Staining the sheets with their dark colours
I kept reaching out for you,
But my arms were burning only in a night
That gathered me into an empty embrace
Until sliding quietly away into dawn,
Leaving its indigo shadows smeared
Beneath the ashy embers of my eyes.

That same year,
You tossed me away with the casual, easy grace
That came so fluidly to your deft hands
And sent me spinning through the Autumn
Exploding in savage reds and orange
That came too late to scald you.

Titanic Expedition, July 1986

And the camera crept like a sea-animal
Through your undisturbed town
Sleeping fitfully beneath a surface
That does not wrinkle with age
But merely sends its ripples out
From year to year;
Unnerving benignity of water
Still folding its calm tentacles
Around you, Titanic and all who went with you
Down to the quietest of water's darkness.

Your crystal chandeliers are eerily illuminated
For the first time since nineteen twelve
As images of you lie flat
Upon the limp pages of newspapers,
And yet, the extravagance of your tragedy
Has lost none of its dimensions.

GERRIT ACHTERBERG

GERRIT ACHTERBERG (1905-1962) is generally regarded as one of the major Dutch poets of this century. In his lifetime, he received all the major literary honours in Holland; and since his death, his collected poems, an oeuvre of over a thousand individual pieces, has gone through many editions. He has been the subject of a wide range of critical studies, and there is a quarterly magazine devoted to Achterberg Studies.

MICHAEL O'LOUGHLIN

MICHAEL O'LOUGHLIN was born in Dublin in 1958. He has published three collections of poetry with Raven: *Stalingrad: The Street Dictionary* (1980), *Atlantic Blues* (1982) and *The Diary of a Silence* (1985), and a critical work, *After Kavanagh* (1985). He has lived for a number of years in Amsterdam and is currently working on a collection of translations of Gerrit Achterberg to be published by Raven in 1987.

TRANSLATOR'S NOTE

That Achterberg has, as of yet, failed to reach a wider audience, is due to a number of factors. The major one is probably the simple inaccessibility of poetry in the Dutch language — which is, in some ways, unjustified, considering the physical and linguistic proximity of Dutch to the English-speaking world. Another factor is the nature of the work itself, which long ago earned the epithet "untranslatable". An Achterberg poem is a piece of verbal alchemy; a slight adjustment in sound or sense, and you are often left with dross. This presents enormous problems for the translator.

Achterberg's poetry has often been seen in terms of the Orphic myth. Each poem is an attempt to recover a Lost Beloved, through the magical power of language. Like a cabbalist, Achterberg seeks to bring the dead back to life by some miraculous combination of words, or even letters. An Achterberg poem often exists on a level of pure verbal performance, the opposite of a vanishing trick. In the poem, a temporal structure, time and death can be repealed. It is this tension between language's ability to "unsay" what has happened, and its inability to actually change it, which gives Achterberg's work its tragic power. In poem after poem, Orpheus tries to bring back his Eurydice — and succeeds, momentarily, through the power of language.

Michael O'Loughlin,
Amsterdam,
1986.

Code

the lifeforce which you once possessed
now spreads itself over the alphabet.
I piece together the keywords from it
and open the heavy lock to your death.

"God" can be represented in verse
by the letters g, o, d,
in this order, but not necessarily,
other formations will also serve.

Every series, any connection
taken from whatever language, will suit
as long as it's at the proper tension.

The poet, while writing, balances his words
for the skirmish of life and death
until the door swings finally open.

Hulshorst

Hulshorst, your name
is like abandoned iron
your station rusts among
the firs and the bitter evergreens;
where the northbound train pulls in with a god-forsaken
screeching,
lets no one off, lets no one on,
o minutes in which I can hear
the gentle fluttering
like an ancient legend from your forests;
grim bands of brigands, rank and crude
out of the white backwoods heart.

Truth

Dead one, I have rotted right down
to the song which I still must write:
nothing eternal can survive
which is not carved into the bone.

I have acquired nothing more than
this cosmic truth; and the assurance
from a number of Dutch gentlemen:
it's a long road which has no turning —

but you are gone.

Blackbird

The early blackbird gargles
goblets of bitter wine:
a dream, which lumps into pain
in the birds' throats
because there is no holding back the dawn;
because the huge integral darkness
can no longer be shut in.

Statue

A body, blind with sleep
Stands up in my embrace.
I feel how it labours.
Death's doll.
I'm an eternity too late.
And where is your heart's beat?

The dense night holds us together,
compacts us of each other.
"For God's sake don't let me go,
my legs have snapped",
you whisper against my breast.

It's as if I bore the world.
And slowly comes the moss
Creeping up over our statue.

Word

You have entered and become the earth.
The rain has sunk down into you;
into you, the snow subsides.
The wind whips you naked.

The light is still in your eyes
As if you had woken this morning.
But they follow neither sun nor moon.
They touch no star.

As far as my blood is concerned
You are sated and replete
With every element.

And yet there must exist a word
which coincides with you.

Geology

Cold is between us
like an ice age, o Man.
You are solid rock.
I am alluvion.

You are state and decree.
I change daily, to become
somewhere, sometime,
new, uncharted territory.

Epitaph

Let me outdie this
with words cooled by death;
they thought, if we kill him
we will strip him of his song.

One day you'll see, on the floor
of my grave, letters of dust:
the song which, rotting, I have become.
But that's no longer any of your business.

JIM NOLAN

JIM NOLAN was born in Waterford where he now lives. His plays include *Round the Garden,* produced by Team in 1981, *The Black Pool,* a prizewinner in the 1984 O.Z. Whitehead Competition, and *The Gods Are Angry Miss Kirk,* premiered by Red Kettle Theatre at The Theatre Royal, Waterford. He is the 1987 Team Theatre Company's writer-in-residence. *The Boathouse* was staged as part of the 1986 Dublin Theatre Festival in the SFX Centre and at various County Council venues, and starred Mary McEvoy, Mary Ryan (Clare), Andrew Connolly (Billy) and Dermond Moore.

The play is set in Ballymountain, a small town bisected by a river. On the outskirts of the town is a disused boathouse, formerely the property of the local boatclub. The location of the play, for the greater part, is here. On the other bank of the river and directly opposite, this building is the site of the replacement boathouse. The action of the play takes place on the afternoon and evening of the last day of the summer schoolterm. The evening marks the occasion of the opening of the new building and for the school-leavers of the town, the disco at the new boathouse will double as a sort of makeshift coming-out party.

The Boathouse: *A wooden shed in poor repair. Where there is paint, it is coloured red. Low railings on two sides, a lifebuoy and a rowing jersey on hooks at back wall on which graffiti is daubed. The shell of a boat, long abandoned, centrestage.*

from THE BOATHOUSE

At the stage of the play at which this extract begins, Clare O'Hanlon and Debbie, both aged 17 and school leavers, who are childhood friends have spent most of the day in the old boathouse. The wilder and more outgoing of the two, Debbie, has tried to but failed to persuade Clare to come to the opening disco for the new clubhouse. Before leaving, Debbie has changed from her school uniform and made a mock scarecrow with it. Evening has now fallen. Billy Ryan, who is eighteen, works in the local tannery.

As the previous scene ends, we hear the last bars of the music from the disco in the new boathouse. As the lights face down to denote the passing of time, the following voice-off is heard from the other side of the river. During this, Clare turns again to the scarecrow. She begins go gather her books and discovering a nailfile in her bag, takes this and going to back wall of pillar, begins to inscribe her name onto the wood. Throughout the following however, she should be seen to be listening to the speeches.

Voice Off: (Chairman of the Boat Club) Ladies and gentlemen! Ladies and Gentlemen, your attention please! We interrupt the proceedings now to come to the serious business of the night. *(Cheers and shouts)* As you know, this evening is an auspicious occasion for the Ballymountain Boat Club, marking as it does, the culmination of several long years of effort in the Campaign for the construction of your marvellous new boathouse. *(Cheers)* Without further ado, it gives me great pleasure to introduce Mr. Michael Ryan T.D., Minister for Sport and Youth Affairs who has kindly consented to perform the opening ceremony. *(Applause).*

Minister: Thank you. Thank you. Reverend Fathers, Reverend Sisters, Mr. Chairman, Ladies and Gentlemen.
The politician's lot is not an easy one. In these recessionary times especially the burden of power weighs heavily on the

58

shoulders of Government. The cyni-cs sneer and the critics jibe, but few realise that the crown of power can so often be a crown of thorns, and that though we wear that crown manfully, the pain of it can sometimes be almost intolerable. All too often, as Government Ministers, we preside over the official closings and not the openings, so much so at times, that some have suggested it is the Government should close and not the factories, ha - ha. *(Silence)*. Yes. Well all the greater therefore was my delight at being asked to come here tonight to perform this happy ceremony and to share in celebration not consolation.

The Ballymountain Boat Club has a proud tradition and deserves to take it's place in the forefront of Irish Rowing history. All around us, in this beautiful building are the silver cups and trophies which are the evidence of that proud tradition. But, if I may be so bold, I have not come here tonight to speak of tradition. I have come to speak not of the past but of the future and of the part this boat club can play in the future development of Bally-mountain.

Mens Sana in Corpore Sane as my old Latin master used to say — a healthy mind is a healthy body. This is a maxim I would heartily commend to you and in particular to the young people of Ballymountain who are here enjoying themselves tonight. *(Cheers)* I understand from the Chairman that for many of you, here present, this evening marks another milestone, the occasion of your leaving school.

It is indeed, I venture to suggest, an interesting and fortuitous conjunction, the occasion of your leavetaking and the opening of this fine boathouse. As Minister for Youth Affairs, I can tell you that my Government is acutely sensitive to the needs and aspiratons of our young people — we will not be found wanting in the challenge to fulfill those needs and those aspirations. That is why I am so pleased to be here in Ballymountain tonight where a real social outlet to the youth of this town is being launched. I would further venture to support that if there were more boat clubs, there would be less mindless vandalism which seems to permeate every corner of this land. We should be proud of our young people and not ashamed. We must provide for them and not deny them, we must celebrate them and not berate them! Let us build more boat clubs! Let us build boat clubs and boxing clubs, running clubs and golf clubs —

Clare: (Interjects quickly) — Coal Clubs and Pudding Clubs —

Minister: Let us turn our country into one giant country club and let us dedicate it all to our wonderful young people! To them I would repeat —

Clare/Minister: Mens Sana in Corpore Sane.

Clare: Row till ye drop!

Minister: It gives me great pleasure to declare the Bally-mountain Boat Club, formally open!

(Cheers and applause. Billy is standing upstage. He applauds ironically, then comes downstage).

Clare: (Surprised). Billy?

Billy: Right first time. Sterling stuff eh?

Clare: It's what they get paid for I suppose. To rally the troops. What are you doing here?

Billy: I was going to ask you the same question.

Clare: Did you not go to the dance?

Billy: For a while. The excitement's too much for me.

Clare: Sounds like quite a party.

Billy: Debbie and you were having one too. A funeral party she said. (Clare turns away). Is it private?

Clare: No. All are welcome.

60

Billy: (Sits by her). Good. I brought me own bottle for the wake.

Clare: Seems to be the night for bottles.

Billy: Well I didn't want to be left out of the celebrations now, did I?

Clare: That wouldn't do. Is Debbie enjoying the dance?

Billy: You know Debbie ...

Clare: Yeah. I don't think she likes me anymore.

Billy: That's putting it mildly.

Clare: Was she talkin' to you?

Billy: That's putting it mildly too. Couldn't get her out of me sight.

Clare: She's mad about you, y'know.

Billy: And she's *mad* with you. D'you want some?

Clare: (Takes bottle) I could do with a drop. It's turning cold.

Billy: (Takes off jacket) Here. With sir's compliments.

Clare: Thanks Billy. I don't blame her. She has every good reason to be mad with me.

Billy: Have you been a bold girl then?

Clare: No — that's the problem. Did she tell you I was here?

Billy: She ... mentioned it.

Clare: And a lot of things besides, I'd say.

Billy: And a lot of other things besides. You here all day?

Clare: A woman died and I went to her funeral.

Billy: The woman from Orchard Street?

Clare: (Surprise) Yes, Did you know her?

Billy: Joe mentioned the funeral, that's all.

Clare: I don't think anybody knew her. You better go back Billy. If Debbie knows you've come over here, she'll slay the two of us.

Billy: Hell hath no fury like a woman scorned. I'm not going back — I get bored at dances.

Clare: Debbie'll be livid. She had plans for you, y'know.

Billy: What sort of plans?

Clare: Like I said, she fancies you.

Billy: Fancy that! (Flick of the hair). Billy Ryan — God's gift to the Ballymountain girls.

Clare: I wouldn't go that far.

Billy: Wouldn't you? (He laughs) Neither would I. Can't live on me good looks and charm forever I suppose.

Clare: I *was* sorry to hear about the tannery, Billy.

Billy: Three days is better than no hide — it could be worse.

Clare: It could be better. You should have asked the Minister for a job.

Billy: Building boat clubs. Mens Sanitary Corporation Sanitorium. Did you *ever* hear the like of it.

Clare: We learnt it in school.

Billy: You learn a lot in school.

Clare: Schools' out though. Debbie says we learn the real lessons now.

Billy: Debbie might be right. You miss it already, don't you.

Clare: School? I suppose I do. The comfort of it.

Billy: No cushions now Clare.

Clare: No cushions now.

Billy: I was scared shitless when I left.

Clare: That's hard to imagine.

Billy: Hard man Billy, but it's true. Like being landed feet first into the water there and told to sink or swim. I can't swim. Can you swim, Clare?

Clare: Debbie can.

Billy: Can you?

Clare: No.

Billy: Doesn't matter. That's what lifebelts are for. Tell you a story Clare, tell you a story about my old man. Years ago our house went on fire — no-one hurt mind, but the place was destroyed. So the fire-brigade is called and I'm despatched to run like the clappers to Brennan's Bar for the oul' fella. The old bugger is moulded onto a bar stool, one hand on his pint and the other proppin' up his jaw bone. So I tell him about the fire, that the house is destroyed and how he better get his ass up to South Street doublequick. Well the fucker doesn't bat an eyelid, but by some great feat manages to move his lips. "Anyone hurt" he says, like he was enquirin' about the health of his favourite pigeon. No, I tell him, there's nobody *hurt* but the fuckin' house is *blitzed!*

So, he says, so what's the *bad* news!

Clare: I don't believe you!

Billy: Cross my heart and hope to die. The Gospel according to Jamesy Ryan. First and only Commandment. Thou shalt not Care! We should go down to Brennans and have a look at him. Sittin' there, sculpted onto the bar stool, starin' into space like some sort of statue he'd mounted in his own honour, and he silently mouthing the words of that single Commandment: Thou shalt not Care.

Clare: Debbie says not to think, your da says not to care. Between the two of them and that stupid Minister, we'll have race of perfect sportsmen and zombies.

Billy: And we'll all live happily ever after. Imagine it Clare, the entire population of Ballymountain out rowing on the water. From Cromwell's Lock to Mount Misery, the whole town on the river rowin' like the clappers from now to eternity.

Clare: With your man, the Minister standin' here with one of them loud hailers, exhorting the troops to Row Till Ye Drop, Row Till Ye Drop.

Billy: Yeah! And my oulfella on the other bank with a placard saying Thou Shalt Not Care, Thou Shalt Not Care.

Clare: They'd soon get fed up of it.

Billy: We'd soon get used to it.

Clare: That's the trouble — I suppose we would. Maybe you should go back now, Billy.

Billy: (Lightly) Are you trying to get rid of me?

Clare: No! No, of course not. Only —

Billy: Only I'll stay so — I'm going to buy a boat.

64

Clare: You must be loaded.

Billy: Money no object. Sail away, never come back.

Clare: Would you like to?

Billy: Sometimes. Yeah, sometimes I would. Would you come with me?

Clare: I might. And I might not.

Billy: I mightn't bring you. Robinson Crusoe wouldn't be half as good if he'd had company.

Clare: He mightn't have got lost in the first place if he had.

Billy: We could go to Guatemala or Madagascar. Send postcards to me father c/o Brennans Bar. (Accent. Reads card) Madagascar Hah! Bloody foreigners! Nothin' but foreigners over there.

Clare: Would you really like to though? Go away I mean?

Billy: I'd like to go sailing. Down to the sea in ships. The tide is out. We'll go tomorrow.

Clare: I've work tomorrow.

Billy: Hackin' mate for the Bull McGrath. Chucks and lime bones a dime a dozen! Cows tongues me speciality.

Clare: Please Billy — I'll have enough of that tomorrow.

Billy: Are you not looking forward to it.

Clare: I can hardly wait.

Billy: It won't be forever Clare. You're made for better things than scrubbin' cows bellies y'know.

Clare: Yuk!

65

Billy: Do y'know why they have three bellies?

Clare: I didn't know they *had* three bellies.

Billy: Yes, you'll have your hands full. One is for starters, one for the main course and one for dessert.

Clare: Very funny.

Billy: Might be funny but it's true. There's very little about the internal mechanics of the cow that William Ryan couldn't enlighten you on.

Clare: I'll know where to go if I'm stuck so.

Billy: Stuck Pigs! Now there's a subject Clare. Did I ever tell you ...

Clare: Shut up Billy.

Billy: Ah I'm only messin'. You'll soon get used to it.

Clare: That seems to be the recipe for success in the big bad world.

Billy: No use complainin' Clare — no one listens. (Bottle) Here. Jamesy Ryan's cure for all ills.

Clare: (Taking bottle). This town is soaked in blood. D'y'know that Billy? I had to see McGrath yesterday about the job and afterwards I got the sort of thinking about blood and meat and things.

Billy: A dangerous subject ...

Clare: There are fourteen butcher shops in Ballymountain. Fourteen butcher shops, two slaughterhouses, a factory that makes glue from the blood of dead horses and a tannery.

Billy: Half a tannery. Three days remember.

Clare: It's a lot of blood though, isn't it?

Billy: Ballyblood.

Clare: Meatstown.

Billy: Bloodymountain.

Clare: Buckets of blood in the streets of Ballymountain.

Billy: Red sails in the sunset, blood on the water.

Clare: Blood *and* water. Two rivers in Ballymountain.

Billy: One of blood.

Clare: And one of water.

(SILENCE)

Billy: (Walks to the riverbank, looks across at town). Thou shalt not care. Thou shalt not consider thyself, thou shalt not give a fuck. (Pause) Maybe the old bugger is right, Clare. Maybe he has it all worked out. Some ... instinct long ago stirred, blinded once by the knowledge that indifference was the only way. Jesus! I should have been a poet! Maybe he saw what you see too Clare, — but he'll never die of anxiety, that's for sure.

Clare: Maybe he's already dead.

Billy: Maybe. (Pause) Do you ... do you ever get frightened Clare?

Clare: Yes ...

Billy: (With difficulty). And ... and lonely.

Clare: Yes. Yes I do.

67

Billy: So do I. (Laughs) Hard man Billy but I do. (Pause) And once ... once Clare, in that stinking factory, beside a stinking pit of hides, I cried my bloody eyes out. (Laughs) There you are now, it's not everyone I'd tell that to, but I did. Because I was so lonely there. And because, me in that stinking pit with old men who'd been there long before me, who'd been there all their lives really and whose skin was beginning to take on the shape and smell of leather. And because they were whistling or singing as they worked and because I knew that if they didn't sing, they'd be crying too. And because I knew a time would come, when I'd be singing too and a time would come when I'd stare into the light as my father does and assume that great indifference too. And because I didn't want to Clare, but in Meatstown, maybe it's the only way.

Clare: Two swans on a summers day.

Billy: What?

Clare: Nothing. There's two rivers in Ballymountain, one of blood and one of water.

Billy: And we can't swim. Not a stroke between us.

Clare: We could learn.

Billy: Then teach me.

Clare: Teach yourself Billy. I'll be there beside you.

GERRY LOOSE

GERRY LOOSE was born in London in 1948 and lived in Co. Kerry until 1983 when he moved to Scotland where he now lives. His poetry has been widely published in magazines and anthologies, and he has had two long poems broadcast on RTE radio as dramatized plays for voices, *Crow Work* (1982) and *Eitgal* (1984), much of which is extracted here.

For some years preceding his death in AD 823, Eitgal was Abbot of the small monastic community on Skellig Michael, a tiny treeless rock 8 miles off the coast of Kerry. Clearly only an unusual man would choose to live in such a situation; only a man driven to proving his faith — confused and passionate. It is equally clear that such a man would be far stranger, more complicated, more a man of his times than the received image of a saintly hermit scholar happy with blackbirds and his white cat.

Any discrepancies or anachronisms in these poems will be found where my knowledge and confusion parallel Eitgal's.

— *Gerry Loose.*

AD 823 Skellig was plundered by the heathen and Eitgal was carried off and he died of hunger on their hands.

— Annals of Innisfallen

from EITGAL

1

Am I not Eitgal, winged fury, wings of wind
the blusterer, the breathmaker, the singer
rising like a head of steam, warlike
the scalder
fletch of Michael, a feather fallen of the
archangel, plume and pennant of Skellig
of Michael, abbot of this sea rock where I am
blown, where I blow
ach a windbag
Christ oh abate you my pride.

2

Wordblind half bard
soured cleric
unchaste monk
succoured futile flesh-stone

3

Are those to the east
the mountains of my youth
passed through for Skellig westward
scald crow hills cloud shadows taking
days to pass, black wings on the
greying rock, lichen shadows growing
on the flanks of mountains
neither slower nor quicker
than moss than black birds than my faith
the passage of a cloud shadow.

4

Notice then how the sun petrifies
the night wet stones, the sea's waves
melt to pudding, my questions borne
down, doubts flattened
felicity in prayer rising
gannet heavy, to fall smack in the sea
leave me staring stupid
work to be done

5

Moan of monkish prayer doleful introspective
to sing Christ in sun days gale days alike
lifting old stones moss stones
with worksong unbidden to the lip
tuneless and tuneful unthought
and thick with now rising over head and ears
as these cells stone on stone
swell and diminish as the work
laborare est orare.

6

These things I see I miss to bend the knee
flying spiders on the wind making that leap
I cannot, peregrinatio, on umbilical abdominal
web line landing anywhere unknown stone or
campion grove.

Small boys chatter, unknowing
words in the face of God
a choir, a falling apart a looseness in the face,
flying, of stiffness.

If the Caolcu, the holy men, the whippet
thin men of Iona, those doves of the church
Colm's darlings, returned here

these silly monks blow me up
seal fed, grain fed, sheltered
yet complain

flutter at them, not at me. Learn
hardship from the north.

Perhaps he serves neighbour best who is not hungry
Christ's men we all are
sin to please the flesh
they pleasure themselves mortifying.

Eitgal is a quern
wordquern grind corn grating men host thin
sacrament; monks for the sacraments of love

I know Mary *I know Mary*

I wear the monks for her
I thresh I grind quern-Eitgal for love
love of the earth
love of the mother
the mother of God.

Eitgal wants a woman
quiescent member tumescent menhir
rock hard rocked into menhir socket
erected with ropes hauled into
soft earth moist mother
exposed to weather
hail flailed crack of lightning

ah the horned god wears my meat.

The brothers get by not loving
some of the brothers desiring
Eitgal loves all
Eitgal wants a soft woman human
no harm in that where's the harm in that
harm to Eitgal
cut it off cut it off.

Pig latin; pork latin
watery snot ridden phlegm
we grunt and snuffle
hawk over our prayers, fatten
out the lean latin
we ate belly of pork
nipples intact on the singed scalded skin.
Pigs.

The night moth, turning aside
stunned by daylight
resting here under this green
by night seeking the sun that terrifies
in weak rushlight
we sing singed by the awful vision
eyes filmed, sancte venite
candles to the dawn.

Saille, little willow, chieftain tree
hawk tree, spring tree

> *Come to me Mary*
> *Come to me Christ*

wind whirl, turn, roll, ear shell, volute, whorl

> *Come to me now*

sallow, wallow, will shroud, corpse mouth bubble

> *Come Mary and Christ*

sally, leap, spring back, resilient salvation

> *Come now*

crack willow, withy, goat willow, sally
white willow, sallow with ears

> *Come to me Mary*
> *Come to me Christ*

Starlight through the cell door.
What is Eitgal. Ten stone animal
aspirant to the Christ
                    ant
on a floating leaf wandering to the edge
and the edge, and back
waving arms upwards, craning, peering
seeking rescue.

Rustic reciter of strange litanies,
mediator, parenthesis among men, monks
animal plodding a perishing wet stone
yet I give thanks.

To the alter prosator, Blathmac of Ia
listen, we're local lads
Gael and Gall of these islands
Eitgal, Darerca, Brendan
Gerald, Kentigern, Uigbald
charity begins here.

Fools perched on little stones in the sea
we squabble for muck
though I hold this earth dear
these pebbles
Skellig, Iona, Colonsay, Aran
Mull and Man
Lindisfarne and Ultima Thule
Hy Brassil and the Orkneys
Alba, Banba, Anglia, Northumbria
are muck without

May God forgive us
we try.

Failbhe had deformed feet
and stood for no nonsense.
Bending the knee
to Feidlimidh the King
his lumpy left pediment
peeped out from his hem.
God! the ugliest foot west
of Jerusalem said Feidlimidh

God is good; I bet, said Failbhe
there is one as ugly much closer;
this looking Feidlimidh straight in the eye
the King (the King) swore and rose and bet
Failbhe rose too and
pushed forward his other crab foot.
It was hard to keep a straight face.

16

Believe me
dropping blood is easy
compared with the horrors
of place
going into the unknown
never again to speak my tongue
to see my folk, hear
the coughing of cattle
in the stall of dawn.
Red martyrdom takes
only foolhardiness, courage
takes only conviction, strength.
For exile, going into the
whiteness
you must know the face of God.

to be sent back with
the oarsman just here

Finian, on this lake island
this testing ground bound by rules toil worn
we are austere, as novices we try hard

to do without fear
for that is to deny faith
we do without sadness
because that is usually self pity

praying, we stand
in cold water like trout; it cleanses us
sleeping, we roost
on rocky ledges like peregrines; it lightens the load

we do without music
though we growl our psalms
we do without meat
though we spice our greens with sorrel
willingly we do without bread
though we crack teeth on stony oats.

But Finian, brother storekeeper
must we also go without ale?

Sluicing down
the rain cannot stop.
Inside for three days
grey days
black prayer
stones above
stare at the page
stare at the wall
the page won't hold
the hand is the letter E gone mad.

Then wakened by light, a strange dog scattering hens
the sun among the clouds, splintered in a thousand
still puddles on the hillside across the valley
spiked and magnified in the drop left on each tasty
looking willow bud, a land rinsed clean.

At the cell door
scrimshanks
arms akimbo
shaven poll
now hear Eitgal's patter stop;
the Word; re made

When I asked Failbhe
how big was heaven,
what was the size of it,
Round about the same size
as the inside of your skull
was his reply.

Do you hear me
my heart my life
half of my soul
the way is hard
and I want to be
ringed by creation
not negation

do you hear me out there
the other side of the glass
rapping tapping
the prison of my days
tit to pit
hear the bubbles
the fish mouthings of my faith

do you hear me
crying from my desert
life, life, love
you asked a word
I answer you
if you hear me
stay away

One day
at last and of course
Failbhe went away
and there was still
work to be finished
if only dreams
though I wept
to think he would never
see the slow green leaves
tongueing spring
this physical temporal
green you eat
with all your senses and heart
that he sorely loved.

And the cat pined
and I move to not
think

Failbhe walking one day
came across a severed head
which he toed.
Wearily, yellow eyed it spoke

Look for nothing
twelve hundred years from now
it will be heard and found strange
and the sound
put in the mouths of others
Always be a free man when you speak
not a slave
Abolish the rich
I have forgotten
what my words mean

WILLIAM RUANE

WILLIAM RUANE was born in Galway in 1960. After living for a short time in London and Germany, he returned to Galway where he became involved in graphics, working on shop fronts, murals and magazine covers. He now lives in Cork.

The three extracts included here are from a longer narrative work in progress, dealing with the problem of incest through the story of a young girl growing up in a small rural Irish town.

Prologue

The pain within that first gentle swelling,
   tightness, in a young throat
   life burrowing in.
Beauty is created then,
   and the beast, lips
   and claws, both scratching at the glass.

Firmly on the ground go christian feet
   and heads buried in the sod, God-like,
Rickety old patriots with dirty medals
   relics,
       a saint's bone, a chip from the true cross,
Umbilical, crushed.

'Discover Ireland'
   it's being sexually abused, fingered,
Petted heavily on a soft celtic night,
   by a father,
Whose heart rises every Easter Sunday, heroic

Pearse, pierce.

Love does not question,
          it seizes
   and it fucks around, faithless.
The bulk heaving brute, maiming
Child,
    plea
      "Daddy, Daddy, NO please."

Why did she think she had no friends?
   we were here, me and you
spitting in each others eyes
waiting for a call,
       from GOD;
"Blessed are the meek"
         because they will not notice.

The Taking

Daddy you stare at me
   from your chair
   at my twelve years.
At my unknowing frame.
You see my woman, small and budding
   and sense my fear.

When Mammy's out
   at her Novenas,
   praying for us all
You watch me from your chair
   and ordered me,
         'Clare, come here.'

I lifted my head from my book
   and look at you, Daddy
You look so strange,
         What's wrong?
'Clare, come here.'

Dutifully I come to you
   and stand there
   meek and afraid.
'You never hug me Daddy,'
   I could have said
Before you grabbed my wrist
   and squeezed my hand against your pants
I would have cried out
   but your hand under my frock
   stifled my narrow scream.

How could I cry
   when I saw you shaking
Oh I had to fall right through the pain
   your brute hand forcing
   your child's own skin
Your eyes cannot look at my face.

83

'Daddy look at how you hurt me.'

And you would push me away
    and throw your head
    and gag.
I thought sometimes, you'd plunge
    through the kitchen window,
I prayed sometimes, that you would.

Daddy I can hear you
    breathing into your fists
Your big bald head is shaking
    are Novenas meant to be like this.
Everytime Mammy's out, I turn into a cripple
    and you stare from your chair that way.
At my fourteen and fifteen years
    and my stifled scream.

Now I tremble everytime
    we're left alone
I listen as your hungry breathing
    fills the room,
And I wait for the command
    muttered from your huge trembling face,
Forgiven by your God
    as you impaled me,
Your own crucified little child
    dying underneath you.

And you damned me as you rose up
    and threw your self aside
As you called out
    with your head buckled.

'Go up to bed Clare, go up to bed at once!'

Your pig authority remained.

I disappeared up to my room
    and cried until my tight screaming brain
Eased itself into sleep.

84

I knew I'd be allowed stay out late tomorrow night,
Friday was your night for Novenas
    and not for crucifying me.

The Rugby Club Dance

Clare,
    no-one knows about the past,
    except you,
            and nobody cares.
Walk along, jacket draped
towards music and lights, coloured
electric pulse moves couples, linked
swaying towards nothing; excitement.
A couple kiss somewhere, a pledge is made
lasting three hours or so.

Amidst the crowd a tall woman slides
syrup clinging dress, a hip rippling
through airy folds, long perfect legs,
                    Strength.
She can make the choice, make men cringe
at a glance, and stub them out,
                    like so many Dunhills.
She knows how weak men are, and can kick
the little boy's balls,
And she does, at a glance,
                    Heroine
Clare admires such strength,
the stone beneath the fleshy fruit
But you, there is no hard or soft
just a space, a lonely hollow.
                    Fill it, fill it!

"Howya, doyawant'dance?" Oh Jesus no, not him again.
"Oh ... well okay so." What can I do?

God this is great he thinks,
I have her now, success
Can feel her underneath, soft, shaking
weak, God it's great, can break her down
Squash her, tear her apart,
                    Love her.
Yeah, yeah, yeah.

'What's wrong here?, this man, macho
is he? he's sort've fat, look.
                    and Jesus he can't dance.
But he's warm, God, what does he want?
I know, I know, but why?
why can't I want, and take,
                    demand like this.'

Every now and then, when rhythms changed
and movements either grew or died,
Big hands squeeze, smudging thumbs
on narrow shoulders.
Big hands leading Clare around the crowded floor.
And as moments slipped he drew her closer, tighter
his chin in her eye,
A clumsy hand moves along her shoulder,
working at it.
Touches her arm, her waist,
                    grasps her there.
                        'Oh God.'
She must not feel, must not.

His big face, purple, looks at her
That she had last seen by the mobile chipper,
Vinegar tainted Estee Lauder,
As Paddy and the boys slobber and devour
Burgers and chips with fingers for forks,
    greasy blinking faces.
His eyes, a squinting smile,
His mouth moves down, and sucks at her face,
                    A kiss.

Sucks at her again.
                DADDY!
            the dancing ends.

A shy retreat, to find her chair
amongst mountains of glasses and lakes of spilt drink.
Her friend Mary, … is gone!
                Jesus No.
She finds her coat and wraps herself.
                He touches her arm
"Clare … areyoualright?…"
"Yeah, fine." Panic. "Mary's gone home. I have to go now, really
it's late, I'll be killed."

"Shure listen, I'll walk you home, it's not safe for you to go
by yourself."
"Oh but really, … I can't …"
"Now listen, not another word, there's no problem. Wait here and I'll
get my coat, alright?"
"… Okay."

As they left the Club he gripped her arm
and led her down the few threadbare, carpeted steps
A soft mist bathed nearby street lights,
suffused, the glittering street,
night wept, quietly.

"Fuck, it's pissing."

A car, overfilled, ached away
from the kerb and headed for home.

"Shure listen, Clare. Why don't we go back to my place. I've a flat
in Church Street, it's only a few hundred yards. It's grand."
"No, I can't. I'll be killed if I don't go home, I don't mind
getting wet."
"Come on, I'll walk you home in a while when it stops, don't worry."
"But, …"

Can there be a greater fear than this.
Men don't listen, ever, none.

'Daddy, never stopped his playing,
fondling, his stinking breath.
His hands squeezing my bottom,
even my wee-wee.
Nobody ever said this wasn't right
nobody ever stopped him, and mammy cried.
Daddy, you hurt me.'

In three minutes they were there, outside
a virtual tenement, a bedsit. God not a bedsit!

The great sodden door creaks in,
a dark hallway is revealed
high ceiling, old floral wallpaper
weeps against the walls,
                    he leads her in.
A damp smell, the door closes.
                    BLACK!

Up they moved, the ancient creaking steps
fingers touching wet walls.
She hears the stairs, and his breathing
Heavy, familiar, his hand pulling her along
Breathing, daddy in the dark,
                    don't slap her again. Please.

A light flashed on.
"Here we are," he said.
They stood before another door,
A number four painted coarsely on one panel.
Its paintwork like the walls was chipped and dirty,
Everything was chipped and dirty.
                    She felt it too.

'What am I doing here? Oh God please help me. This bastard, I know
what he wants. What's he going to do, Oh God.'

He put a key in number four and turned it.
"Well there you go, it's not much, a bit on the small side ..."

'Jesus, I can't believe that she's here.
What will I do now? Christ, get down to it I suppose.
Take it slowly, no need to rush things is there?
I'll bring her home then. Yeah well ... '

"Eh, sit down ... anywhere."
There was nowhere to sit apart from the bed.
        Clare sat there.
He sat beside her, looked at her stockings, legs,
        embarrassed and lost.
"Well now," he gazed at her face, *"this is grand."*
        Minutes drifted.
His two big hands reached up
and caught her face, wet hair.
He stretched his neck and kissed her small sealed mouth,
moved closer. His right hand held the back of her head
and he squeezed his tongue between her teeth. She sat there, afraid.
He pushed her slowly down, rubbed her small, cold breasts,
tongue shoving, a hand rubbed her side and her thigh.
His mouth slobbered, he pushed himself against her.
"Jesus Clare, you're a lovely girl, lovely."
Clare was crying now.
"Please Paddy stop, please. I've to go home, please."
"Oh Clare, it's grand shure, grand, lovely, ..."

His mouth comes again, dribbling, sucking her wet face.
A hand, huge, moves on her thigh, going underneath, searching.
"Oh Jesus Paddy stop."
His body was shaking now, can't stop
hand feeling softness, warmth, pushing
searching still. She's crying.
"Listen Clare, take these off, it's okay, please, take them off."
Clare, silent now, can't feel, crying, can't feel.
Her flower hand covers her face, can't feel.
"Clare ..."
His hand, fingers prying, finds a grip
peels down tights and knickers, everything slides away.

89

Her shoes clatter on the floor. He has her now,
he lifts her feet onto the bed.
'Oh she's lovely, Jesus Christ.'
He's standing up quickly, trembling, his pants open,
panic, fumbling hands. His pants gone,
everything throbbing, huge, wet,
he feels her, crying
"Oh Jesus, Clare."
He lies on top of her, grunting, sweat
Inside, huge, pumping
"Oh lovely, Jesus ..."
She's not here any longer, cried away
wet hair in her eyes, she sees the ceiling,
bare bulb dangling, cobwebs, connecting
strands, a spider watches from its den
the animal violation.
He's heaving, still faster. She sees his huge face
vessels gorged, sweat dripping on her breasts.
His stretched head, grinding spasm
Tearing flesh, sucking head, Meat Animal, crunching.
She sees his mouth, slobber, her flesh,
   Her flesh a burger
Grinding, pumping, her flesh, his leering face
Fresh burger, his burger eating face,
   She sees his mouth,
      She's smiling.
His burger eating face she sees, she giggles
         His face, Jesus!
She's laughing now, breath short, ringing.
                  He sees her, giggle, giggle
He stops, he stares at her, she giggles,
No moving, nothing, he looks
"FUCK YOU! Bitch, bitch," ashamed he slides away.
                  He slaps her.
"Ye bitch, whatareyelaughin at, ... ye fuckin' whore,
whatsfuckinwrong?"
He grabs her arms, pulls her. *"Comon ya bitch, Out, ... fuckinOu*
He drags her off the bed, banging on the floor
Across the tiny room he pulls her
"What'swrong whatwhatwhatyadirtywhore?"

90

He pulls her by the hair, she staggers on her knees.
"Out, ya bitch."

He throws her towards the door, roaring
"OUT!"
lips spitting, eyes frantic, roaring.

Quickly, quickly she moves,
grabs her tights, wet shoes, knickers.
Tears streaming, hurting, raw.
He pushed her out, *"Bitch, mad bitch!"*
into the pitch dark landing.
   He slammed the door.
     Black.
She stands there, weeping
small hands clutching her mess.
Damp clothes, tears, ... smiling
              in the dark.
One hand touches a wet wall, slips on her shoes blindly
the stairs, black, a step, down.
No love, can't feel, no soul,
        just pain.

'What's wrong with me?
I can't feel ... anything.'

Daddy shook the soul out of her
   his fingers squeezing, mad red eyes.
Daddy, is this love? ... is it?
         Stumbles in the hall.

Paddy, poor old Paddy,
buckled on his narrow bed
his tiny room, shrunken,
        insignificant.
'She laughed, Jesus why?' his pale, wet face.
'What a thing to do ... laugh, Jesus what did I do.
She's a crazy little bitch anyway, Christ.'
       The front door slammed. She's gone.

Poor old Paddy rises slowly, walks across the tiny room.
He pisses into the little sink, gushing yellow
Member in hand, sticky, red
Dwarfed by dirty fingers. *"She laughed at me."*
The tiny voice ringing,
        "Jesus I can't even ... laughed?"

In the little town, pitifully wet
hungry lives huddled together,
Under thin roofs, eyes, slits against the dust
against the seeping dawn.

    "Rejoice, rejoice
    our lost boys have returned,
    With warm blood on their hands
      and a song in their hearts.

    We have been waiting,
            all our lives."

BILL TINLEY

BILL TINLEY was born in Chicago in 1965 and has been living in Wicklow since 1970. He is currently a student in Maynooth College. These are his first poems to be published.

Electric Heater

Where the bedclothes are stale with recent sleep
and the air sucked bloodless by cigarettes,
nothing breathes but a silence, lung-filling.
In a room, you watch electrically,
radiantly, a flow in the blackness,
red coil of instant death, locked in a cage.
Companionship does not come in words, talk
or even a warm touch in the winter.
It is skin-close, tangible as the sky.

Like a friend who goes away forever,
you must die. Washed and cold you disappear.
As stream water held too long in cupped hands,
you have sapped out of this dark communion,
cracking, snapping, like knocks on a steel door.
The senseless streetlight pokes at my curtains,
a fool who does not understand hatred.
An opening key grinds in the doorlock.
Voices cut like daggers from the stairs.

September

I Morning

Morning forms over fields of rain-downed crop.
I have work to do and cannot stop
Too long to watch this age awaited birth.
The reek of water-blackened, nightfed earth
Is stronger than intoxicating sleep,
The cock-crow call of waking hillside sheep
And diminished orchestra of the trees
Filters down this autumn's infant breeze.
The stonewall moss is damp beneath my hand,
Worming birds flock and rise up from the land;
And through the mist of dew drop drying out
The mountains clear. Morning fills my mouth,
Invades and captures forest, farm and fern.
Satisfied, I go to work. The child is born.

II Evening

Smelling of smoke, frosted air rushes
Inside my nose, stream water slushes
Slow over stones. Breezeless evening.
Sunless. Only dull light lingering
Across dark fields. Under that blue chill
The eye strains for detail on black hills,
My ears recall the white crashing froth
Of winter's savage floods. That worn wrath
Is now a calm gurgle in autumn;
Yet an anger gathers in the hum
Of dying flies. The pitch parachute
Of darkness falls as thick as clogged soot.
Cold replaces warmth and I oblige
The flies by surrendering their bridge.

Moon

Bared skull-top of darkness. Faceless. Fleshless.
Bleached turn of bone in the deep sky.
Hung like a globed lantern
And snuffed with a licked pinch of cloud,
Ritual of reflection — untallowed, wickedness.

You feast with a hunger for miracles
In the wet palms of pitch bog pools,
sunk to an unshook white
In this eternal alchemy
And fondled like sin in the mud liquids of turf.

You sleep like well-fed fish, mute water owls
Tucked under tussocked, breaking banks,
Rolled to new shades of change.
Thirst slaked and fattened, brothers until dawn,
You lie in no particular fraternity.

Then slow, swung like a pendulum, you become one again,
And vanish into your ephemeral kingdoms of night.

Cyclops

Cyclops of the day I call you.
One burning eye, rising, falling
Back through the branches you enslaved,
Into lakes and ditches with your fire.
This island is your empire, master —
Close one eye, the world walks blind.

Cyclops of the room I made you.
Eye of bulben glass and tungsten,
Switch survival in a socket,
Copper wire veins, electron blood.
This island is our empire, comrade —
Close the eye in harmony.

Cyclops of the mind I main you.
Cell-like eye, you focus and fade,
You struggle in this shut-down show,
Flounder in this dark, unfingered fluid.
This island is my empire, servant —
Stab the eye, death falls through a dream.

Rabbit

Just a swift brush of fur-brown in the night
And not, thank God, a pillar steeled with fear.
Don't look back, rabbit, as you career
Ditchwards in the euphoria of flight,
For am I not your new gomorrah lure,
The eyes of death into which you must gaze?
Let your lunatic heart pump wild in praise
And rejoice in fields spread with warm manure.

Must I now salt old wounds for you again?
Recall a fogged night lamped among stone walls,
Mad laughter that terrorized your brethren.
Never cold enough to kill, guilt swells
Flood-like in the calm rivers of my brain.
You escape, drunk with life, through the soft rain.

Apology

Night has bound blacker than deep water
and now is that repose, storm breeder.
Lights from town are latted on the lake
soft as silence. Old pride is at stake.

We crunch over gravel, the cold crack
like the breaking of a beetle's back,
and cooled by the scent of evergreen trees,
embrace; it's time to apologize.

A Sort Of Victory

The lights were going out in houses
From here to where it was already dark,
Just the pipe-banging radiators
Grumbled from under the drawn curtains.
This was the time to best observe the world —
When sleep had slumbered everyone.
When house-moths wing-tapped the kitchen light
And nightwind knocked at the ill-fit door.

There was a time for sleep a time ago.
Now I've found the treasure of the dark
With a table-lamp and an old pen,
On pages pulled from musty closets..
The radio had died its daily death
On the crumb-rough counter by the sink;
Our cats will claw dry putty from the glass
For milk that's soured in their saucers.

In awe of this opportunity
I am powerless to appreciate,
Like a thousand prayers offered up
For miracles you don't believe in.
The pen lies stubborn by the paper,
My mind sets solid in this strange stone —
Aspiration is the pure pleasure,
Victory's only pain. I surrender.

FERDIA MAC ANNA

FERDIA MAC ANNA was born in Dublin in 1955. He has made his living as a musician and journalist, and these scenes from 'Cartoon City' — a novel in progress — are his first published work of fiction.

Scenes *from* CARTOON CITY

1. EDDIE REGAN

The Lord plucks neon from every city on earth and showers it on O'Connell St. He puts yellows in the burger joints, white on the movie marquees and pinks and reds in all the amusement halls. The street photographers with their blue camera flashes he adds as a gag.

People wait in clumps along the traffic islands, shooting jets of steam breath at each other as they raise arms to flag down taxis which rarely stop. Couples glide past, wind-scorched faces snuggled together, peeking out to avoid the rowdy and wayward drunks. Scatters of young men, eyes brimming with alcohol and night air, conquer pavements and ford traffic lanes, husky voices battlecrying. Outside the darkened cinemas and burbling burger joints stand the oddly assorted spillings, those finishing off the pub arguments and those waiting for a chance to start one. On a bench in the main traffic island, by the statue of Daniel O'Connell, a drunk lies with his feet up against the railing, baying out Frank Sinatra.

Eddie picks his way along, immersing himself in the sights and sounds of a city that has changed much. He remembers a brighter, slower place where the light from the shop windows and street-lamps played across the silver bumpers of smiling cars and sparkled on the tops of bus stops and rubbish bins. Now the dark congeals in deep pools in the middle of the road, spreads out from the cover of doorways, collects in the avenues between the parked cars and floats like a cape along the alleyways and sidestreets.

Faces surge about him, footsteps clip-clopping concrete, dislocated voices returning to him like the babble of beach transistors. Dodge City, he thinks, all you need is the covered wagons and horse riders.

Up ahead a gaggle of young men break suddenly into a screaming run, flying past with ferocious good humour carved upon chalk faces. One shouts at Eddie as he goes by, arms thrown wide as if to snatch him off his feet. Before Eddie can raise a hand the young man is gone, snapping off across the street in a headlong

101

rush, bootheels clicking and arms flapping for take-off. Laughter cuts the air like razors.

Eddie feels angry at first; he wants to tear after them and smash his fists into their sharp young mushes; do them in one by one. Then, the anger subsides and is replaced by weariness; a realisation that he is stranded without direction, reserves or sufficient time; things come along, toy with him briefly and then leave him plonked there, rooted in the middle of the footpath with a stupid expression.

And now there is a new sound he has never noticed before: the smashing of glass, dull, distant and always emanating from somewhere behind him. Whenever he turns he sees nothing, merely feels the aftersound hanging in the air like the echoes of a siren.

He holds his collar closed and walks.

At the corner of Parnell street he passes a man and a woman barging at one another, the man waving his arms in the air. As he crosses the road there is the crack of a slap.

Outside the doorway of The National Ballroom on Parnell Square a cluster of men stand exchanging comments with two monkey-suited doormen. Eddie can make out the Dublin accents but none of the words.

He walks head down, chin into his collar against the wind, hands in pockets, suddenly on the lookout for the finger of glowing orange that denotes the cruising taxi.

He finds one at the corner, climbs into the back, settles into crackling plastic with his hands stiff in pockets. He gives the driver Katie's address and sits shivering, gaze straight ahead seeing everything the driver sees without taking any of it in.

At O'Connell bridge the taxi stops to allow a tinker girl to lead a sturdy, brown-and-white speckled horse across. On the horse sits a small tinker boy with freckled face, staring down at the cab, perching like a High King. From the horse's shaggy rear-end hangs a red neon tail-light, put there by the Lord, just for gas.

2. KATIE DOOLAN

'So I met him in Tara Street station and we went out to Howth on the Dart train; he woulda had his brother's car only his brother needed it himself and he couldn't get the loan of another one so the Dart train it was. It was OK too. I had never seen the city from above like that before or at least not the way you saw it as you looked down at all the houses and the boats tied up, at the back of Boland's mills there, you know it was like bein' on a plane. Anyway it was gas for a while but then you get a bit bored with the whole thing, especially when he was just sittin' there the whole time like a wax dummy, the face on him pointed out the window seein' nothin', starin' inta space and seein' nothin'. I'd lean over to him and say look Eddie and show him some sight but he'd just nod and say yeah fine fine I see it and then keep on bein' the way he was before. It nearly drove me bananas.

Then a mother and a young Boy sat down opposite us. The mother was tryin' to stop the boy from messin' but the youngfella wouldn't stop. She kept smilin' over at us to show us that she knew what she was doin' but the youngfella was walkin' all over her, climbin' on the seats, pullin' outa her. So then the train turned the corner into one of the little stations, Howth Junction I think it was, and all of a sudden it gave a jerk, just when this kid was at his worst, and the next thing you know this youngfella took off outa the seat just like he was flung and landed in the aisle on top of some woman's bag of groceries, scatterin' them all over the gaff. So the mother got up and picked up her kid and the other woman got up to gather her groceries and they both started shoutin' at each other and the kid was bawlin' and the train was stopped at the station with all passengers gettin' in and seein' this commotion first thing. It was like a scene out of a looney bin.

But it made Eddie laugh. It made me laugh too and I couldn't stop even though the mother was glarin' at me, I just couldn't help myself. I don't know how it happened but I looked down and there was Eddie's hand holdin' mine. I must have gone beetroot. Maybe seein' that little child flyin' through the air just made his day. Good job that the mother took the little brat home at the next stop

103

otherwise I'd say herself and Eddie woulda dug trenches in each other.

He held me hand all the way to Howth and we even managed a conversation. He asked me did I remember the last time we came out to Howth together and I said that I did, only too well. I remembered all his mates liftin' the barrels of beer outa the back of some pub on the hill and loadin' up Davy Masterson's car with them, I told him I remembered that alright and there was a lot more I could recall that I'd rather forget. He laughed at that, sayin' it was all part of growin' up. I said it was all part of gettin' sent away but that only seemed to make him happier.

When we got to Howth we waited outside the station for the single-decker red bus that goes up to the summit. The station-master told us it wasn't late very often but that there was a new driver on the route and he sometimes took longer than the regular fellas. So we stood out in the cold and waited, Eddie lookin' all around him as if he'd landed on a new planet which, in a way, I suppose you could say he had after being inside and all. I left him there after a few minutes it was so cold, I told him I'd wait in the railway station and he told me to go ahead, he'd give me a shout when the bus came. I watched him out of the window and he was walkin' up and down in the freezin' cold, his coat flappin' off him, lookin' at everythin' as if it was the first time he'd seen trees and grass and smelt sea air in his whole life.

It made me sad up there lookin' out at him, I kept thinkin' he was gettin' old all of a sudden, even though he's only twenty-nine or thereabouts; he looked as if this was as far as he was goin' to get, this was where it all ended one way or another. He'd give me a smile now and again, one of those pixie grins he's famous for and for a moment the clock'd be turned back and it'd be four years ago. It made me feel hopeless . . . it seemed like every time Eddie and me went out there'd be some moment or other when all the hopelessness would shine through. I've met him three times since he's come out and every time it's the same, in the pub a couple of nights ago, the other day for that snack we had . . . and then yesterday, waitin' at that station in Howth for that little red bus to come and take us up the hill to visit all the sights we used to enjoy when we were young lovers or sweethearts or whatever we used to call ourselves. . . I knew it would never be the same, I knew he'd never stay workin' with his brother . . .

104

somethin' was bound to happen . . . So when I heard the whistle and looked out and saw him grinnin' up at me and that little red bus beginnin' to turn the corner into the station driveway I knew that the second I walked out that door I was tellin' him one big lie, pretendin' that things could work out for us, not lettin' on to him that I knew that somethin' was goin' to mess them up, no matter what we promised each other.

We sat in the back seat, the way we used to, and stared out at the view as we climbed the hill. Except for some of the modern houses you'd swear you were back in the dark ages, y'know, viking times. Eddie said they should build all the houses one on top of the other, just like a block of flats, that way you'd only have one ugly part of the place to deal with and the rest would be natural and wild. He said all the blocks should be stuck on the other side of the hill where only the ships at sea would see them and that the only other houses that should be allowed were the ones down in the village and around by the harbour, as long as they were old houses and not these new yokes. It was OK to have pubs all over the place though, because with all these beautiful views around it was obvious that people would do a lot more walkin' around than they did at the moment and it was important that there were sufficient drinking establishments about in order to quench the considerable thirst that would be created as a result. The world according to Eddie Regan I told him.

All the fun we had on the way up the hill. We were the only passengers, sittin' right down the back like a pair of young eejits, lookin' back out the window at the road windin' down into the greenery and the harbour beyond with the sea lashin' up against the piers and the fishin' boats bouncin' up and down softly on all that blueness — small flecks of white burstin' through all over it, like tiny dollops of cream on one of those wobbly jellys — you'd have thought we were the only people on the whole hill and that the bus driver was our chauffeur for the day.

When we got out of sight of the harbour Eddie held my hand again. I kept tryin' not to look into his eyes in case he'd see what was up with me but the truth was I was gettin' more content every minute, not wantin' to get off the bus, not ever, as long as the feelin' kept gettin' better.

Eddie told me about the work he was doin' with his brother. He told me they were goin' to make a good few bob if it all turned out OK, and they were both sure it would. I only half listened to him, I was starin' at me shoes, thinkin' about another pair I had at home that would have been much better matched to me jeans. But he didn't notice, he kept on yappin'. I suppose I made him feel comfortable, secure — maybe he thought everything was just as it was before.

At the summit we got off the bus and stepped into this hurricane. We had to walk all the way up to the top of the hill with the wind whippin' the clothes off our backs. Eddie didn't seem to mind at all. He laughed every time he saw the look on my face. Once he grabbed me and held me close when a big gust came but he let me go immediately after. He didn't even notice whether I wanted him to keep holdin' on or not. I remember the sky was purple, with all these dark grey clouds scrabblin' in over us in a hurry from seaward, I thought we were goin' to be drownded but it didn't rain, not even a drop. Maybe it should have.

There were no cars at all when we got to the top; it just wasn't that kind of day, and so we went up to the little wall by the cliff walk and jumped over. There was a gate of course but we never used it in the old days so we didn't now — it was like declarin' we were back, you know?

The wind from the cliffs blew my hair back against my head until I thought it was goin' to tear it out by the roots. I had to squint me eyes against it, I could scarcely see where I was goin' even then. Out of the corner of me eye I saw Eddie laughing at me.

You look like a masthead off one of those old-time ships he says, desperately tryin' to find its way back to the ocean. Very funny I says. Either that, he says, or you look like you're gonna turn into a kite and take off. I says, you'd love that wouldn't you, the wind knockin' me over and makin' me look a fool. It's doin' OK as it is, he says to me. And it was too, I could barely keep me feet.

We walked as far as we could without the wind blowin' us out to sea. Half of me was lovin' it and the other half wanted to get sick. Then do ye know what he said to me? He told me he wished we could be a couple of gliders that the wind would blow way out into the waves where they'd sink underneath for ever, with not a trace to be found. I told him he was carryin' on again, that as far as I was concerned I was only up here with him because I felt sorry for him and not because of some huge, unfinished love affair. But he only laughed at me again.

106

When we turned around to walk back I felt him put his arm around me but I dodged it off. After we climbed the little wall and got out of the brunt of the wind he tried again and this time I had to pull his hands off.

What's the matter, he says, all worried looking and innocent. You're the matter I tell him. It's all right he says, you know I won't hurt ye, I never hurt ye, I was only puttin' me arms round ye.

I stood away from him as he rattled on about how it was a new start for him and how he was goin' to do fine now that he and his brother were gettin' along so well and all that. I started cryin' when he talked about the old days — I had me back to him so he couldn't see me, and even if he had he probably woulda thought it was the wind — he went on and on as if we had both agreed to get married or run away together or somethin' — it was awful, the tears just kept on.

Then of course I started to shake, and jesus he noticed that because he broke off talkin' in the middle of some crap about gettin' a house and came over and grabbed me by the shoulders. What's wrong he says, what's wrong, over and over again until I couldn't stand it anymore and I turned round and smashed him into the face with me fist. I hit him so hard he went flyin' backwards. I went after him shoutin' and roarin' about everythin', hittin' him into the face again and again, watchin' the shocked expression in his eyes, goin' after him as the knees began to buckle under him. He ended up against the wall — I'd say he'd have fallen only for that — and I laid into him with all I had, calling him an eejit and a bastard and flyin' at him with both hands until his nose started pumpin' blood. He got this look on his face once he put his hands up to his nose and saw the blood — as if someone suddenly plugged him into a socket — he grabbed both my hands and squeezed them until it hurt, starin' at me all the time ready to cut me heart out if I so much as blinked. Then he threw me from him and turned away, wiping his nose with his sleeve. I stood there for a long while, sobbin' an' bawlin', afraid to look at him. All I wanted to do was cry and keep on cryin' until it was all gone outa me.

I don't know how long it was before I stopped but when I did he was beside me, holdin' on to me arm and leadin' me gently down the hill. It was hard to keep my feet at first but he steadied me all the way. I didn't look at him once all the way down to the bus stop.

107

It took ages for the bus to come. We stood sheltered in the doorway of a house beside the bus stop, just across the road from the pub where we used to go for a drink after we'd do the cliff walk. He said nothin' and neither did I. I had this sharp pain in me nose after all the cryin', I had to keep rubbin' it to try and ease the pain. Eddie had his hands in his pockets, he leaned against the door with his back to me.

We got the bus when it did eventually decide to come and we caught the Dart train back to town. On the way I saw Eddie's face properly. There were tiny streaks of blood along the sides of his nostrils. On the skin beside his left eye there was a red mark where one of my nails must have caught him. It made his face look middle-aged. We spend the whole journey in silence except for around half-way when I leaned over to him and told him I was sorry. He took no notice of me at all.

When we arrived at Tara Street we walked together as far as the ticket gate then he quickened his step suddenly and got a few places ahead of me in the queue. By the time I passed through the gate he was gone, taken off down the tunnel and out of the entrance into the city, swallowed up. He'd left me to the station like a gentleman should and then, when he was sure I'd be alright on my own, he cleared off rapid.

So I walked home by myself. Sure enough I got drenched. I didn't care, just kept walkin' until I got home, put the key in the lock, came in, threw off me wet things and jumped straight into bed. I would have cried had I any tears left but I hadn't. I lay there in the dark and thought the whole business out about ten thousand times. It did no good at all.

I keep rememberin' the way he looked at me when he grabbed me that time, his eyes locked into me, it must have been the way he looked that day when he had his barney with the coppers. It's all there just beneath the surface. I can bring it out of him any time I want. But I wish I hadn't. I wish we hadn't gone up to Howth, I wish we hadn't had that scene on the hill. Maybe if I hadn't hit him . . . I wish they'd never let the bastard out.'

3. CARTOON CITY

The building stood whitewashed on the corner, criss-crossed by black wooden beams, a long metal sign over the door splashed with the head of a crowing cock in crimson advertising 'O'Neills bar and lounge — Quality Drinks!' At the side, rising through the whiteness like a scar, a rusting fire escape zig-zagged its way upwards, terminating under the pot-planted windowsill of the third floor.

Opposite the fire escape was a small garage, its cars spilling onto the narrow street and around the corner into the laneway. Mechanics, oily in blue overalls, buzzed and bent, hammered and clattered, catcalling their way through the morning. A radio gabbled from within, pumping out exploding drumbeats and whirring keyboards. The music flitted across the road to the base of the fire escape, twirled around the reddened iron framework, pitter-patted up the step-grills, skirted the sharp bends and penetrated the third floor window to the small one-roomed flat where Eddie was making love to Katie on cloudy bedsheets, his lower body jerking in rhythmic percussion, each thrust tumbling more of the purple eiderdown onto the floor where it uncoiled with feathersoft precision.

He fucked her without looking at her, without the slightest sign that he knew who she was or cared what was happening to her. Three times she turned his head to face her and three times he shifted his gaze so that he focused upon the top of her head, the pillows on either side, or some undefined spot between the bedstead and the wall. He conducted his assault upon her in one prolonged campaign punctuated by brief pauses for regrouping and realignment. She clung to him, gasping when he hurt her suddenly, biting her lip to absorb every crumb on offer, digging her nails into his back during the awkward stops, low breath punched out of her in steady time. Every time she dug her nails in he thrust harder into her and every time he thrust harder she dug her nails deeper and made hollow soothing sounds.

He came with a small snort and hung upon her, his back and legs stiffened while she held him tight. Then he rolled off and lay with his back to her, settling into the sheets while his breathing grew quiet.

She lay feeling empty and unfinished, one hand splayed loosely against the small of his back.

He fidgeted for a moment then began to drum his fingers off the mattress. Katie curled up against his back, feeling the tension build in him.

Finally he erupted off the bed onto the floor. He grabbed his trousers and stepped into them, giving little jumps in the air to push each foot through. Sweeping up socks and shirt and jumper he headed towards the door. Katie watched, curled up and silent. She stretched out and rescued the eiderdown from the floor, pulling its crumpled heap slowly over her until only her face appeared. He kept his back to her while he dressed at the door. When he finished he opened the door and stepped through. She heard him plod a few steps and then pick the telephone receiver from the wallphone.

'Christ shite,' he said, and there was the creak of returning footsteps before he appeared in the doorway again.

'Tenpence for the phone,' he said, his gaze not meeting hers.

Her slim arm emerged over the top of the eiderdown, bent like an angle-poise lamp and indicated the windowsill. 'My purse on the ledge.' She retracted the arm and drew the warmth up under her chin as she watched him cross the floor to the windowsill and search in her purse, short fingers poking and shuffling. He found what he was looking for and tossed the purse back on the sill. It toppled off onto the floor like a dead soldier. 'Right,' he said, and walked out.

'Don't mention it,' Katie said softly. She turned over and wrapped herself deeper into the eiderdown.

Through the open doorway she could hear dialing noises and then the coin clang as he pressed the 'A' button. The voice was low and she could only make out the odd word or phrase. For a moment she thought he might be ringing the police to turn himself in but then she heard him laugh, a rumbling wheeze like a balloon draining. She snuggled closer into the warmth and tried to block out the mumble from the corridor. From outside the window came the sound of shouts and laughter and the sharp slap of a football being kicked against concrete. A male voice, deep and throaty, was bellowing an invitation; 'come on, have a go, come on.' There was another sharp slap and more laughter.

For a minute she lay and allowed herself to drift away. The

110

sounds of reverie steered her thoughts to childhood and schooldays
and long summers when there was nothing better to do than run
up and down dusty streets, yelling like a little demon. She dismissed
all remembrances of actual events from that time and concentrated
instead on recalling the feeling of living always for the present, free
of all prospects, or worries, or responsibilities. Enough of the feeling
filtered back for her to give a small smile and hug herself under
the eiderdown.

When she looked up there was Eddie standing there, a totem
pole with a furry face.

'I'm goin' out for a while,' he said. The Moores want their smack
back, I have to set somethin' up.' He sat on the ground and began
to pull on his shoes. 'Ye better ring in sick today and tomorra.'

'They're not expecting me today. I have to go in tomorrow.'

Eddie tied his shoelaces. He finished and stood up suddenly.
'Just ring in, I need ye to make it work. It'll all be fine and ye won't
have to work in that stupid fuckin' job anymore, just think about
that.'

'I don't want to be involved.'

'YE ARE FUCKIN' INVOLVED. STOP GIVIN' ME FUCKIN'
PRESSURE I'M TRYIN' TO LOOK AFTER US AN' YOU'RE
GIVIN' ME FUCKIN' PRESSURE.'

She huddled away. When she spoke again he cut her off, his
voice stroking pussycats.

'I ask ye to do one thing for me — one thing, somethin' that's
goin' to help us both and now you're kickin' up — I'm goin' to
haul ye outa this kip and give ye what ye've always wanted and
ye can't even see it starin' ye in the fuckin' face. Wake up woman
for fuck's sake.'

'I'm wide awake. It's you who won't wake up.'

Katie sat up in the bed and put her head in her hands. She held
the eiderdown in place with her elbows. Eddie looked at her in
disgust and walked to the door, bending to retrieve his black coat
en route. 'Now ye're fuckin' cryin'.'

'I'm not cryin.' I'm never goin' to cry again.'

'Then what are ye fuckin' doin'? This is our one fuckin' chance,
if we don't take it it's over D'YE HEAR ME IT'S OVER, THE
WHOLE FUCKIN' GAME, EVERYTHIN'. THIS IS THE BEST
WE'VE GOT SO WAKE FUCKIN' UP.'

He opened the door and paused. 'Your trouble is ye don't know what ye want.'

'I know what I don't want. I don't want more trouble.'

'Oh Jesus,' he said, 'what's the fuckin' point. Look I'm under pressure. You're supposed to help right? So why don't ye fuckin' help me. Ye'll be helpin' yerself too.'

Katie was silent. Eddie stared at her. 'I'll be back soon, get ready will ye? and stop bawlin' it does no-one any good.'

'I'm not bawlin',' she said.

He looked at her but she didn't move. He closed the door with a slam.

She waited until she heard his footsteps disappear and then threw the eiderdown from her and reached over to the floor. She scrambled in the mess of clothes until she found one of her own shoes which, straightening up, she threw at the door with all her strength. It hit with a thump and dropped. 'Haaaa,' she yelled.

She lay back on the bed and wiped the tear tracks from her face. Then she placed her hand on the light tuft of hair between her legs and began to stroke, up and down, in gentle movements, purging the pain and anger, soothing away the confusion. She closed her eyes and listened again to the slap of the football from outside. Gradually the sounds melted into the rhythm and her childhood feelings returned, bringing with them sensations of sunshine and dust and of something new and unexpected, around the corner.